The Maintenance Partnership Relationship
The Key to all Successful Asset Management Programs

T0312950

Published 2024 by River Publishers

River Publishers

Alsbjergvej 10, 9260 Gistrup, Denmark

www.riverpublishers.com

Distributed exclusively by Routledge

605 Third Avenue, New York, NY 10017, USA

4 Park Square, Milton Park, Abingdon, Oxon OX14 4RN

The Maintenance Partnership Relationship / by Kenneth E. Bannister.

© 2024 River Publishers. All rights reserved. No part of this publication may be reproduced, stored in a retrieval systems, or transmitted in any form or by any means, mechanical, photocopying, recording or otherwise, without prior written permission of the publishers.

Routledge is an imprint of the Taylor & Francis Group, an informa business

ISBN 978-87-7004-228-4 (paperback)

ISBN 978-87-7004-636-7 (online)

ISBN 978-87-7004-627-5 (ebook master)

A Publication in the River Publishers Series in Rapids

While every effort is made to provide dependable information, the publisher, authors, and editors cannot be held responsible for any errors or omissions.

The Maintenance Partnership Relationship

The Key to all Successful Asset Management Programs

Kenneth E. Bannister

Canada

Routledge
Taylor & Francis Group

NEW YORK AND LONDON

Contents

Preface

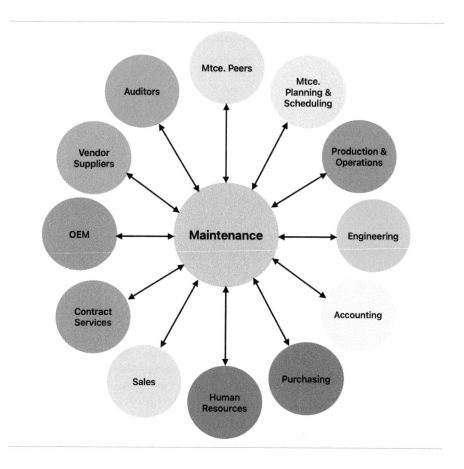

Success in any walk of life is dependent on partner relationships. A successful marriage is based on a relationship in which both partners collectively embrace their similarities, whilst they collaborate to use each other strengths to overcome weaknesses and bridge their differences. Where teams are concerned, there will be many partner relationships that will need to be navigated and managed separately to achieve a defined and unified level of success.

Take for example a race car team. Success, or the seasonal goal, may vary based on a mix of past performance, changes made, and the current perceived performance ability of the car and team ability to work together toward the stated common goal. In this scenario the goal may be to finish the season as the series champion, or in a designated grouping such as top five placement, or top 50% of the field. This will require the driver to not only drive the car at peak performance, but also develop a partnership with the mechanics to relay the car's changing performance and condition at all times to make timely changes to the car; develop a partnership with the engineering and design team to continually improve the vehicle design; develop a relationship with the team manager to understand and assist with team strategy; develop a relationship with the team trainer to ensure a level of fitness required to drive the car at peak performance.

The relationship model described above is parallel to all successful team efforts and is no different to the relationship model requirements of the maintenance team as it strives to achieve a best-in-class approach to asset management.

According to the Encarta dictionary, a partnership is described as:

1. The relationship between two or more people or organizations that are involved in or share the same activity,
2. Cooperation between people or groups working together,
3. An organization formed by two or more people or groups to work together for some purpose.

On any single day, a maintainer must interact multiple times with internal and external resource partners to perform their job. To function professionally, a maintenance department must set up and manage multiple partnerships on a continual basis. Partnerships are relationships that live or die based on an understanding of the input and output communications and tangible deliverables required from both sides to make quality management decisions, and enable each partner to consistently deliver on their performance mandate at minimum cost.

Figure 1 demonstrates how the maintenance department has three specific partner relationship types. Depending on the organization setup a maintenance department can be structured internally with a planning scheduling department, a lubrication team, a predictive maintenance team

Figure 1: Maintenance departmental partner relationship model.

and an inventory and tool management team. This internal maintenance department structure relies on intra-departmental partner relationships to function efficiently as a service provider. Within the corporation, the maintenance department must rely on inter-departmental partner relationships to ensure it funded sufficiently and is provided with all of the required operational resources. Finally, the maintenance department requires external partner relationships to supplement its internal resource requirements and meet its regulatory requirements.

Before maintenance can assess each relationship individually and determine suitable input/output matrices, it must first assess and understand what it can, and cannot, manage on a daily basis. Table 1 depicts major equipment downtimes attributable to maintenance and non-maintenance causes.

Maintenance caused downtime incidences are the direct responsibility of the maintenance department and its maintainers. Maintenance programs must be set up to work diligently on reducing/eliminating these types of downtime incidences. The non-maintenance caused downtime incidences are out of the direct control jurisdiction of the maintenance department – even though maintenance is charged with the indirect responsibility of restoring equipment uptime after a non-maintenance incidence has taken place.

Table 1: Reasons for major equipment downtime.

Maintenance caused	Non-maintenance caused
• Ineffective lubrication	• Operator error
• Incomplete repairs	• Sabotage
• Ineffective PMS	• Lack of equipment access
• Poor maintenance scheduling	• Exceeding production design limits
• Lack of parts	• Poor housekeeping
• Lack of knowledge, training	• Not informing maintenance soon enough
• Lack of tools	• Lack of available parts
• Poor communication	• Lack of asset availability

Unfortunately, many maintenance departments do not track and distinguish between maintenance related and non-related downtime incidences and render themselves easy targets to take blame for all downtime occurrences.

Implementing an effective planning and scheduling program, and targeted training and certification programs, alongside a best practice lubrication management program, will reduce many of the direct maintenance related downtime causes. Whilst partnering with in-house and external consulting partnerships to gain control of its direct maintenance caused issues, maintenance must also work on its relationships with indirect partners to significantly reduce their impact on the maintenance budget by setting up a report system that classifies all related and non-related downtime incidences, their impact on operation throughput levels, impact on maintainability and product quality issues, and deliver these reports on a regular basis to their appropriate partners. This is best achieved through effective communication in which accumulated data from work orders, condition monitoring, and predictive trending reports are synthesized and converted into management information that can be understood by the partner (outputs). For example, management may only need a conceptual "big picture" synopsis of the situation, whereas purchasing or human resources may require a more detailed account of the situation. Conversely, maintenance must also inform its partners of what information (inputs) it expects in return, how often, in what form, and validate how the information will be used. Often, many partners are blissfully unaware of their impact until informed by a maintenance department report indicating the consequences of their actions.

On any given day the maintenance department can expect to interact with up to twelve groups from within and outside the corporate organization. In a manufacturing or plant engineering environment, maintenance can expect to interact most with production, engineering, accounting, and purchasing departments, and to a lesser extent with contractors, customers, vendors, human resources, quality, IT, and management. Table 2 shows a sampling of inputs and outputs required with many different partners on a typical day in which the inputs are deliverables from the partner to the maintenance department, and outputs are deliverables from maintenance to their partners. In her book *Leadership and the New Science: Discovering Order in a Chaotic World*, management guru Margaret Wheatley states: "In organizations, real power and energy is generated through relationships. This pattern of relationships and the capacities to form them are more important than tasks, functions, roles and positions."

For the maintenance group to truly succeed in its mission to deliver asset availability and reliability with a decreasing skilled resource base, it must establish improved working relationships on three levels: (1) intra-departmentally among clerical staff, planners, schedulers, inventory stockkeepers and managers; (2) inter-departmentally among equipment operators, production supervisors, production planners, engineers, purchasers, accounting, human resources and all management personnel; and (3) intimacy with the maintainable assets.

Building these vital relationships begins with understanding what you manage versus what you control. For example, a maintenance department is responsible for managing all equipment repairs. Unfortunately, it is not always able to control access to the equipment (operator, production planner, production scheduler, production manager); control access to parts (purchaser, vendors); or control access to funds (accounting, management). Instead, it must depend on mutual working relationships with others to deliver the maintenance mandate.

In any relationship, both sides have different needs and must work together to establish, document and develop areas in which cooperation is required, establishing mutual agreement(s) to prioritize actions based on the consequences of ignoring those needs—*all of which must also be based on facts, not assumptions*. Similarly, we must review the relationships formed with the physical asset.

Table 2: Maintenance partnership requirements on any given day.

Partner	Input to maintenance	Output from maintenance
Production	• Production schedule • Maintenance windows • Asset performance issues	• Maintenance schedule • Equipment readiness • First-time timely repair
Engineering	• Asset specifications • Asset/system drawings	• Equipment performance • Component performance
Accounting	• Vendor/contractor payment	• Cost reports • Budget reports
Purchasing	• Purchased goods • Parts expediting	• Parts specification • Vendor performance
Management	• Department expectations	• Department performance • Department requirements
Quality	• Quality standards • Tooling replacement/change schedule	• Machine operation to specification • First time quality
Sales	• Capacity forecast	• Uptime • Equipment availability
Vendors	• Timely delivery of parts • Timely delivery of services	• Vendor performance • Request for quotation
IT	• Report building • Calibration	• IT system performance
HR	• Training opportunities • New hires	• Training requirements • Employee performance
Contractors	• Availability • Quotations	• Contractor performance

B.F. Skinner, in his book *Contingencies of Reinforcement*, wrote, "The real problem is not whether machines think, but whether men do." In the area of reliability-centered maintenance (RCM), we're taught to understand each of our machines intimately, as well as understand their idiosyncratic nature within their operating context alongside the how and consequence of every possible failure that could occur.

Modern technology allows us to take an intimate look at equipment health – through oil analysis, infrared thermography, vibration analysis, ultrasonic analysis, historical failure analysis, etc. Ultimately, regardless of how "smart" the equipment may be, we still must do the thinking for the equipment and work collaboratively with our peers, management and vendors to ensure we address the machine's needs in a timely manner while still meeting the needs of the maintenance department and its various relationship partners.

Building relationships allows both partners to state their respective points of view—and teaches us not to make assumptions on each other's behalf. Understanding, measuring and tracking what we control lets us objectively define how and where the partnership must work to better manage and resolve issues that are out of our control, or those we must simply manage.

Relationship-building is key to dispelling hurtful assumptions, as well as to delivering a value-added, best-practice maintenance approach in an ever-changing world. This purpose of this book is to discover and review the many relationships that maintenance will need to foster on a daily basis if it is to truly become best in class. The following chapters will offer insight and practical solutions for building and putting place a best practice asset management program based on mutual understanding and relationship excellence.

Effective relationships in which each partner understands their role and influence on their partners success are crucial to any organizational success, even more so today as the corporate and manufacturing world recovers from some devasting years in the early 2020s. Much of the material in this book is derived and updated from a series of original columns and articles I wrote and published over a number of years in *Maintenance Technology Magazine* and *Efficient Plant Magazine.* As a successful award-winning Asset Management Consultant for over 35 years implementing change in many industry environments, I attribute the greatest client successes to those who adopted a partner relational model from the onset of their change journey, I wish you great success on your change journey.

Kenneth E. Bannister, 2024

About the Author

Kenneth E. Bannister is a UK technical apprenticed and accredited mechanical design engineer, credited on several engineering patents, two of which involved tribology aspects in their design. Ken is also a CMRP - Certified Maintenance Reliability Professional and since 1988 has consulted worldwide helping clients implement practical and meaningful asset management, reliability, and lubrication management programs. Ken is one of a handful asset management consultants holding expertise and accreditation in the field of tribology, lubrication failure management and industrial lubrication application as a designated professional MLE - Machinery Lubrication Engineer.

Ken was the first consultant to assist a company through the ISO 55001 asset management certification process in North America and was the key architect in the development of the ICML 55® world lubrication standard. More recently Ken was a contributing author and senior editor for the compilation of the ICML 55.0, ICML 55.1, and ICML 55.2 standards documents.

Practical Lubrication for Industrial Facilities – Fourth Edition, is Ken's fourth industrial lubrication book. In addition, Ken also provided the lubrication section for the *Machinery's Handbook* and has published other books on energy management and predictive maintenance. Throughout his career Ken has published over 650 articles and white papers for numerous international maintenance magazines, with over half dedicated to the field of practical lubrication.

Ken was a founding board member of the Plant Engineering Maintenance Association of Canada (PEMAC) and currently sits on the board of directors for the International Council for Machinery Lubrication (ICML) responsible for the ICML 55® world lubrication standard.

1

Preparing for Partnership

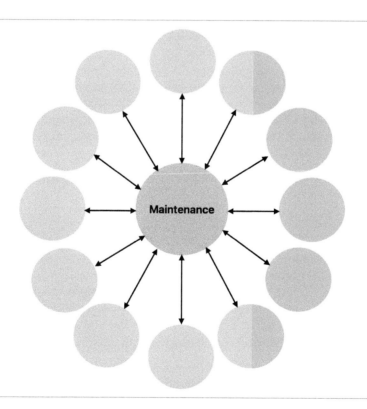

Maintenance departments cannot function autonomously, they need to establish themselves as an integral part of the manufacturing, service and corporate process. As partnership interaction grows, so does mutual understanding, value and respect for each partner's role in the daily work process.

Establishing a valued working partner relationship requires the maintenance department to proactively identify and solicit each potential partner to deliver an investment statement that details the role(s) of the individual partners and outline the mutual benefits of each partnership (inputs and outputs). In order for the potential partner to "buy in" to the concept, maintenance must, from the onset, establish its ability to consistently provide the necessary outputs to its partner, and more importantly, show that it has the mechanisms and capability to process inputs and turn them into equipment availability, reliability, throughput and quality deliverables.

Continued success ultimately is borne out of each partner feeling valued in the relationship. Therefore, if maintenance is to solicit a partner relationship, it must prepare for partnership by understanding its current strengths and improvement opportunities and by ensuring that a successful communication process is in place.

Such behavior is the hallmark of a successful, responsible maintenance department who recognize they must collaborate with and contribute toward the needs and requirements of other corporate departments, while at at the same time being cognizant of maintenance needs and requirements being responsible to itself. This level of behavior and partnership preparation can be achieved using a five-step process (see Table 1-1).

Step 1. Know thyself: Perform a maintenance operation effectiveness review (MOER)

Forging a winning maintenance team is the simple result of understanding and communication. Many maintenance departments struggle with the concept of system management, job planning and open information sharing, often thinking it is much easier to revert to the "path of least resistance" found in a reactive environment based on personal agendas and limited responsibility. Unfortunately, this type of environment fosters low morale accompanied with complaints of lack of respect from both peers and inter-departmental workers.

The first step to breaking free from such a regime is to engage a reputable third-party maintenance expert to audit your current state of maintenance operations. The resulting MOER must recognize staffing strengths and current best practices that can be capitalized upon to bridge the disconnected management areas that present themselves as improvement opportunities. The MOER must address the following areas:

- Planning and scheduling
- Workflow management
- Lubrication management
- Inventory control
- Failure prevention and analysis
- Performance analysis reporting
- Management/partner reporting.

Recognizing, and taking on responsibility for, both strengths and weaknesses is the first step in building an understanding of how the maintenance department and its partners impact each another in the current state, and how partnerships can be improved upon to better the future state.

Step 2. Know thy future: Build an engineered maintenance improvement management action plan

A management action plan (MAP) is a detailed project plan that plots a time lined series of maintenance improvement initiatives determined by studying the corporate and department vision, short-term and long-term goals and objectives, budgets and investment returns. Conclusions can then be drawn so that a phased implementation of projects that can capitalize on strengths and add measurable value to the maintenance function can be drawn up and implemented within a specific timeframe.

Building a management action plan (MAP) requires maintenance to work in partnership with other departments and management to determine the validity of the project. This is the first showcase for maintenance – *and it will set the stage for partnership interaction later.*

Step 3. Develop intra-departmental communication tools

The announcement and commencement of any major maintenance management initiative can act as a change catalyst to develop a crucial intra-departmental communication toolset. This also presents a perfect opportunity to forge the maintenance group into a unified team of peers by involving them in the communication development process. Typical communication tools should include the following:

Table 1.1: Five step process to partnership improvement.

STEP	ACTION
1	Know Thyself: Perform a Maintenance Operation Effectiveness Review (MOER)
2	Know Thy Future: Build an Engineered Maintenance Improvement Management Action Plan
3	Develop Intra-Departmental Communication Tools
4	Develop the Partnership Input/Output Matrix
5	Meet Your Pilot Partners!

- Minimum information requirements to raise a work order
- Work order flow for differing work order types
- Taking out and restocking MRO inventory parts
- Work order design
- Work order fault codes
- Cross shift information transfer notes and status
- Key performance indicators (KPIs)
- Condition-based response actions
- Basic maintenance management system (MMS) failure reports.

There are many communication tools that can be added to the list; allowing maintainers to be involved in the process can assure any immediate communication shortcomings are addressed. The ability to effectively communicate intra-departmentally will show partners that maintenance has the ability to consistently provide outputs to help them – and the ability to act on the input information provided by them.

Step 4. Develop the partnership input/output matrix

The maintenance improvement initiatives set out in the management action plan will require the collaboration of multiple partners to achieve success. For example, any one project could involve management to endorse the project, accounting to release funds, purchasing to buy in product and/or services on time, production to release pilot machinery for testing, engineering to prepare/change specifications, vendors and contractors to provide delivery of goods and services, etc.

The first input/output model can be built to assist in the first improvement project – *and can be approached and presented as a pilot for future partnership dealings.*

Step 5. Meet your pilot partners!

This step is about preparing your case for partnership; it will capitalize on the work performed in the first four steps to instill partner confidence. Be prepared to defend the merits of your new approach – *and to explain why this approach is better than any previous initiative because you now understand yourself and how you fit within the corporation.*

2

Intra-departmental Partnership Maintenance Peers

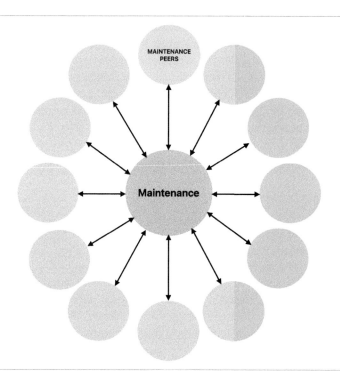

Equipment maintenance problems do not belong to the maintenance manager; equipment maintenance problems do not belong to the maintainer;

equipment maintenance problems, once accepted for investigation and repair by the maintenance department, belong to the entire maintenance team.

One of the hallmarks of a successful maintenance operation is its cognitive ability to recognize and responsibly manage its customers' needs and requirements, and its own. Today's maintainer usually is well aware of the benefits of teamwork wherein the sum of the whole – *or combined team strength* – surpasses any person's individual strength. Ask any maintainer who has belonged to a "winning team" in the past about that experience and he/she usually will characterize it as nothing less than "magical."

So, if teamwork and its benefits are so desirable, why isn't every maintenance department consciously striving to develop a winning team-based approach? The answer is simple. In any form of chaotic working environment, *devoid of any process or procedure*, in which individual maintainers operate autonomously, acting as their own parts buyers, planners and schedulers, it is extremely difficult to find time to communicate with and relate to maintenance peers in a proactive manner.

The benefits of teamwork can only be reaped through understanding, recognition of need to change and structured peer communication. By allowing and encouraging an open communication environment, acknowledging and capitalizing on each other's strengths and working toward clearly defined goals, we can foster true teamwork. Peer connection – *or intra-departmental communication* – is vital for maintenance department success, which precedes and provides the essential ingredient for successful partnership relationships addressed throughout this book.

Promoting Peer Connection

Many maintenance departments struggle with the concepts of system management, job planning/scheduling and open information sharing. Sometimes they appear content to simply fall back into a known path of working in a total reactive environment based on personal agendas and limited responsibility. Under such regimes, cliques that encourage maintenance individuals or groups to work against one another are often formed. When this happens, all maintainers complain of lack of respect and low morale.

Breaking out of a destructive pattern like this calls for a time-lined, structured maintenance management program that recognizes both the present and future state of maintenance. This type of program incorporates a management action plan to achieve both corporate and maintenance department goals within a stated timeframe. Any maintenance management program implemented along these lines will promote peer interactivity through the following:

- **Building on existing knowledge:** Industrial equipment is idiosyncratic in nature; similar equipment will perform differently dependent upon usage patterns and maintenance history. Certain maintainers become expert at understanding this idiosyncratic nature and are able to diagnose and repair specific equipment problems faster than others. Involving these individuals and their expertise in a PM optimization program harnesses and shares their unique understanding of certain equipment pieces in the development of meaningful PM job tasks. Allowing them to build the program in conjunction with other maintainers opens up a forum for the sharing of strengths and knowledge, and provides an arena for informal peer training sessions. The result is a consistent maintenance approach based on the equipment's needs in its working environment and a shared responsibility among all maintainers.
- **Sharing of failure information:** Implementation and utilization of fault or failure analysis programs enable maintainers to succinctly define and share equipment failure data with one another. Defining and capturing failure information on closed work enables maintainers to research equipment history and quickly determine if the equipment failure is repetitive or not. This in turn, allows the maintainer to better perform a planned repair at the root cause level, thereby reducing downtime and eliminating unnecessary repairs.
- **Adopting a consistent approach:** Working together to develop policies, standard operating procedures (SOPs) and standardized work processes allows the maintenance group to work and bond as a team, to develop consistency and trust in each other's approach to the maintenance process.
- **Promoting peer interaction:** New communication tools (e-mail, CMMS, white boards, etc.), increased self-esteem and pride in workmanship all work to promote peer interaction at shift changeover time when work is passed from one shift to the next shift. Efficient work completion and improved work quality are more likely to result with improved shift changeover communications.
- **Setting and surpassing goals and targets:** With a management action plan in place, maintenance successes can be tangibly tracked and reported to management. Nothing stimulates both self-esteem and respect more than being on a successful winning team, which in turn promotes healthy dialogue and the open sharing of information among peers.

Figure 2.1: Maintenance peer partner relationship.

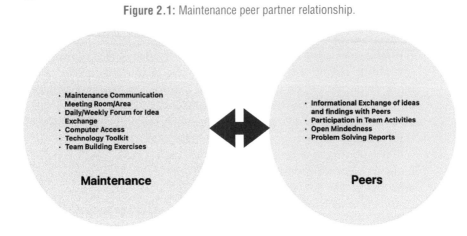

If maintenance problems are to be successfully resolved, it will be accomplished most efficiently through departmental teamwork, promoted by a healthy peer partnership (Figure 2.1).

Intra-departmental Partnership Maintenance and Maintenance Planning/Scheduling Group

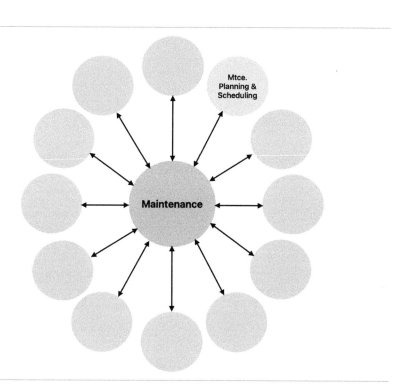

Within the maintenance department there are numerous intra-departmental relationships that are crucial to the success of the maintenance department as a whole, none is more critical than the partner relationship between the maintenance foreperson, maintenance technician and the maintenance planning and scheduling group.

The maintenance planning and scheduling group is a group within the maintenance department responsible for planning each maintenance job, aligning the resources to perform the job, and placing that job on a daily work schedule in a timely manner. The planning function is a specialized job that is performed by a trained maintenance planner and entails assessing work requests, from which are built detailed job plans to perform the work complete with work instructions, parts, tools and safety requirements. Figure 3.1 shows an example of a detailed work instruction based on a best practice go/no go checklist methodology.

Scheduling work requires a totally different skill set. Larger organizations will have dedicated a maintenance scheduler(s) in place responsible for partnering with the maintenance foreperson(s) for each trade group and production supervisor to organization the availability of the asset and workforce to schedule a timeslot for the work to be performed in a timely manner. Within smaller organizations, the scheduling function may fall on the trade supervisor, or be performed by a combined planner/scheduler position in which the planner is trained to perform both functions.

Figure 3.1: Typical best practice go/no-go checklist style work order instruction set for an ac unit filter change. Courtesy: ENGTECH Industries Inc.

Sequence	Procedure	Completed	No-Go
1	Lock out unit		■
2	Vacuum all dust and debris from unit		■
3	Empty and wash condensate pan/drain line assembly, ensuring drain line is free of blockage		■
4	Replace air filter		■
	CHECK:	■	
5	Is the glycol charge sufficient to operate the unit?		
6	Remove Lock out		■
7	Startup unit and run for 5 minutes		
	CHECK while running:	■	
8	Is the electrical system ammeter needle positioned in the operation zone depicted on the gauge glass?		
9	Shutdown unit and cycle on/off 2 times		■
10	Does unit manually cycle on/off without problems?		
11	Complete all sections of work order including relevant comment		■

This high level of connectivity between the maintainer, the planner/scheduler and the client is evident even in a minor, seemingly insignificant, preventive maintenance event such as a simple oil and filter change. Quarterbacking the event is usually the role of the maintenance planner/scheduler, who is, arguably, the most important person(s) within the maintenance and operations groups. It is the planner/scheduler who controls the field of play with a series of connective actions that must take place to ensure the successful completion of any maintenance event.

On any given day within an organization, thousands of decisions are made. Reaching any single decision calls for a series of connective actions or events linked together via established business processes that predetermine at what point a decision is required to make the next connection. For example, a simple PM event requiring an oil and filter change requires the planner/scheduler to set up and execute the PM in three distinctive stages.

Stage 1: Oil change PM event set-up

To execute his/her job correctly with regard to any planned or unplanned maintenance event, a planner/scheduler must develop an initial job or work plan that describes the actions needed to complete the intended event. This simple chronology of work requires the planner/scheduler to connect with the engineering department, the machine manufacturer (equipment manuals), and/or the lubricant supplier—depending on the best resource, to determine the required lubricant, the filter(s), the recommended change-out procedure, change-out interval, safety requirements, and time estimate to complete the work in order to put together a repeatable, executable, engineered work plan.

Figure 3.2: PM event set-up partner connections.

Once the work plan is established and entered into the computerized maintenance management system (CMMS), materials must be ordered and placed in stock, which requires the maintenance planner/scheduler to connect and partner with the maintenance inventory control person, who in turn connects with the purchasing agent, who in turn connects with the material supplier. Figure 3.2 graphically depicts the relational hand-offs for the event set-up process. If the material supplier is a new one, the purchasing agent must also connect with the accounting department to set up invoicing and payment schedules.

Once materials are shipped and received, the receiver connects with the inventory control person, who in turn reconnects with the planner to advise that the oil-change materials are now in stock – *and the department can move on to Stage 2, in which the event can now be scheduled.*

Stage 2: The maintenance event

To perform the event, the maintenance planner/scheduler must now connect with the applicable trades foreperson, who in turn connects with the technician who will perform the oil and filter change. The technician proceeds to the inventory crib and connects with the inventory control person to gather the oil and filter materials.

Figure 3.3: The maintenance event connections.

Then, it's off to the jobsite, where the technician may or may not need to connect with the production supervisor and/or operator to receive control of the equipment on which to work. Once the oil change is completed, the technician again connects with the production supervisor and/or operator to return control of the equipment, then reconnects with his/her own direct supervisor to deliver the completed work order. Figure 3.3 graphically depicts the relational hand-offs for the actual maintenance event.

Stage 3: Paperwork completion

With the event completed and equipment available for work, the maintenance planner/scheduler may choose to connect with the trades supervisor and/or the production foreman and/or equipment operator to perform a work-quality check. Confirming that the work is completed satisfactorily, the maintenance planner/scheduler then connects with the CMMS coordinator or clerk (if applicable), to have the work order closed and filed within the CMMS. Figure 3.4 graphically depicts the relational hand-offs to complete the event paperwork.

During the performance of the oil change, should the technician find a problem requiring additional attention, they will connect with the trades

Figure 3.4: The paperwork completion connections.

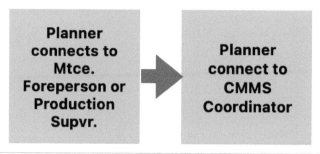

supervisor to discuss the matter or write down the requirements on the work order. The trades supervisor once again connects with the planner/scheduler to discuss the new or additional work requirements, after which the planner/scheduler repeats the entire connection cycle by commencing with the new work requirement at Stage 1.

The Power of Connection

What we see in this scenario calls to mind the lyrics of an old song: "The knee bone's connected to the thigh bone, the thigh bone's connected to the hip bone, the hip bone's connected to the…". A series of purposeful connective and relational events involving both maintenance and non-maintenance department personnel are charted for a simple oil and filter change. Setting up and executing this simple event requires a minimum 16 individual hand-off connections to take place, all carefully orchestrated by the maintenance planner/scheduler.

The connection path will change according to the availability of repair parts, tools, trained resources, equipment availability, communication tools, etc. How smooth that path is will depend greatly on the systems and business processes already in place, at both the departmental and organizational levels, and on the organizational ability of the planner/scheduler.

With this kind of connective power, it is easy to understand those who conjecture that a good maintenance planner/scheduler may be equivalent to three technicians! Such is the power of relation connections!

Inter-departmental Relationship Maintenance, and Production and Operations Group

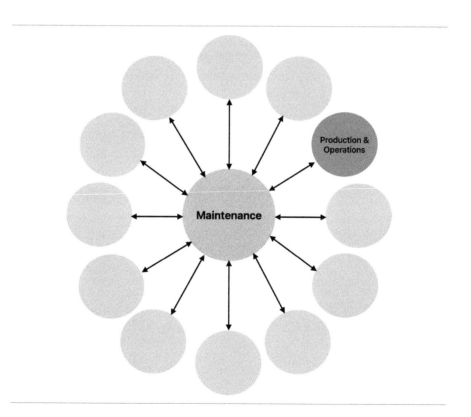

Arguably, the most important relationship in any interdepartmental relationship in any industrial operation is the connection that exists between the maintenance group and the production/operations group. Often viewed as a bittersweet accord, both teams often struggle to define their roles. For those who do manage to do so and build a working relationship, the results are often spectacular, being recognized as a hallmark of a world-class organization.

In order to synergize energies and work together as a unified manufacturing team, both maintenance and production/operations must realize and accept the fact that "maintenance is as integral to the production process as production is to the maintenance process." This statement underpins all of today's major management methodologies, including total productive maintenance (TPM), reliability centered maintenance (RCM), total quality management (TQM), ISO 9000, ISO 55001, etc.

The premise is simple, to achieve maximum equipment availability and reliability, maintenance must be proactive and work with operations to develop an engineered maintenance approach that respects operations' need to deliver high-quality product at a consistent rate of throughput. This calls for development of a reliability program in conjunction with the operations team, as opposed to the old maintenance approach of building a preventive program in isolation and expecting operations to cooperate without understanding the maintenance process or position.

Maintenance is as integral to the production process as production

is to the maintenance process

Traditionally, maintenance has been poor at communicating the "why", and the "how" of the maintenance process, and is often considered to be ignorant of operations' needs, the vice versa also being true! Building a combined proactive approach to reliability allows operations to understand why equipment needs to be monitored and maintained on a regular basis. At the same time, maintenance learns to appreciate problems from the operations side.

Examining the typical complaints from both partners' perspective can lead a workable approach that allows both departments to focus their efforts on the equipment's ability to produce consistent product without taxation.

The following comments reflect some of the complaints voiced by both maintenance and operations.

Scenario 1

Operations: *"A machine is only broken when it can't produce parts anymore!"*

Maintenance: *"Operations will only hand over equipment for scheduled maintenance once it dies."*

Solution...

Defining failure is the first task in building a reliability-based approach to equipment management. In TQM and RCM, the key performance measurement for success is overall equipment effectiveness (OEE) that views the relationship of equipment availability, rate of manufacturing throughput and rate of product quality. OEE will suffer terribly if maintenance is not allowed to ensure that the equipment is capable of manufacturing product at its minimum specified rate of product throughput, just as it will if operations continue to operate the equipment in an obvious state of disrepair. Both scenarios adversely affect quality and are indicative of a partner relationship breakdown. Setting and defining an agreeable minimum rate of throughput that is well within the design specification of the machine, and working together on a strategy to consistently achieve a higher measure, is the first stage in combating catastrophic equipment failure, production slowdowns and poor quality. This minimum machine throughput rate becomes the threshold failure point at which both teams mobilize together as a partnership focused on machine health.

Scenario 2

Operations: *"We can't afford to shut down operations to allow maintenance to perform PM."*

Maintenance: *"We couldn't get the equipment, so we will perform PM on the next PM cycle."*

Solution...

Preventive maintenance should not be an intrusive operation requiring equipment shutdown and lockout to perform simple PM tasks. Utilizing a perimeter-based maintenance approach, equipment can be redesigned for minimum cost to be more interactive, allowing both operations and maintenance to perform rudimentary PM without slowing or stopping production. Figure 4.1 demonstrates a rotary casting table that must be shut

Figure 4.1: Rotary casting table with manual lubrication pump located inside a safety lock out zone. Courtesy: ENGTECH Industries Inc.

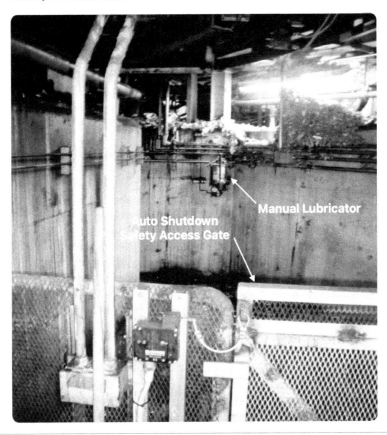

down and locked out in order to manually operate the lubricator pump handle or fill the reservoir. Changing the lubricator pump to an automated pump unit and mounting the unit on the outside of the safety gate system would make the lubrication operation safer, and resolve any partner friction between operations and maintenance arising from machine stoppages for lubrication purposes.

All visual checks of fluid levels, performance output (gauges) and cleanliness levels can be set up with visual management devices set up to reflect pre-determined levels of variance acceptability. Thus, the person performing the checking only need take action if a no-go (out-of-acceptable variance) state is found; predictive maintenance can be set up for remote sampling at the machine's perimeter.

With a partnership approach and a reliability focus, the old way of performing overhaul maintenance can be virtually eliminated, allowing new thinking toward scheduled maintenance requirements that will include subassembly cassette-style component replacement and instant accessibility from 30-second articulated guarding. Working together to determine agreeable time slots for performing short-burst planned maintenance events will allow development of a "pit-stop" maintenance-style approach.

Scenario 3

Operations: *"Downtime is a maintenance problem, not a production problem!"*

Maintenance: *"We always get the blame for equipment downtime!"*

Solution...

Deflecting and placing blame is a favorite human pastime. Taking ownership and being accountable requires us to determine what we are responsible for and managing that part of the equation, while advising those responsible for the areas we cannot manage of their current status. Maintenance cannot, and does not, manage everything that affects its daily operation. Through development of fault codes used on work order completion, equipment failures can quickly be categorized into maintenance and non-maintenance related failures. Specific non-maintenance related failures, such as waiting for production, operator error, raw material blockage, etc., can be reported and communicated to the production team.

Scenario 4

Operations: *"When we try to tell maintenance about a machine problem, they ignore us!"*

Maintenance: *"Production doesn't know anything about maintenance."*

Solution...

Operators instinctively know when their machines are no longer operating within the "sweet spot," but often are unable to successfully articulate the problem to maintenance who can quickly lose patience and choose to ignore their production partner's complaints. In setting up a proactive approach by working together as a partnership, many early detection failure warning signs and events can be pre-determined and written in a language that is understandable (and trainable) to all current and new operators and maintainers. This new machine language then can be tied into the evaluation of when a failed state is near or has occurred.

Defining Roles

Role definition is crucial if both maintenance and production departments are to strike an accord and work in an autonomous, yet cohesive manner to deliver a high-quality product in a waste-free, cost-effective manner. Virtually every major management philosophy and methodology in practice today recognizes and fosters the integral relationship between the maintenance and production departments. Zero inventory based just-in-time (JIT) and lean-manufacturing methods would not be possible without high levels of equipment reliability and availability, driven by active operator involvement in the maintenance process.

Autonomous operator-based maintenance is foundational to the total productive maintenance (TPM) philosophy, and is a cornerstone of the reliability centered maintenance (RCM) methodology, both of which heavily utilize a relationship with the production operators input to design, implement and continuously improve equipment maintenance reliability strategies. Increasing reliability and throughput requires maintenance and production to work together as partners on a two-pronged management and hourly workforce level.

Operator-based Maintenance

Operator-based maintenance can be implemented through the following three-step approach designed to promote confidence in both parties:

Step 1: Commence with a revised work acceptance procedure. Whenever production calls in a machine issue to its maintenance partner, maintenance must guide the caller(s) to disclose their name, the machine #/description, location, area of the problem (component or system) and a STILL (smell, touch, intuition, look, listen) primary sense indication/analysis of what the operator may initially perceive to be the cause of the problem.

Machine operators instinctively know when their equipment is not running in the "sweet spot," but are rarely asked for their opinion(s). This simple action can significantly accelerate the pre-planning process and allow the scheduler to more accurately dispatch the correct resources the first time. If you own a car and have had it serviced or repaired at a garage or dealership lately, think back to your initial conversation with the receiving technician. The technician is aware that you as the operator have sensed there is a problem as the car is no longer acting "normal" to you. They will likely have questioned you in regard to the STILL indicators you are experiencing and under what driving condition they occur. Through experience with the machine or model of car in this case, they can often gather enough information to pre-diagnose and put together a work ticket for repair complete with an initial cost and schedule date for the client. If the problem is not initially apparent, at least an investigative work order using the identified symptoms can be used to quickly identify the root cause and a suitable repair strategy.

Step 2: Allow and encourage machine operators to be part of the testing, start-up and acceptance procedures after repair completion.

Step 3: Introduce reliability centered maintenance (RCM). Choose a suitable RCM pilot and always include the relevant equipment operator and supervisor as part of the RCM analysis team when performing the failure mode effect analysis (FMEA) and condition-based maintenance work tasks. Use a perimeter-based maintenance approach in which the equipment is set up for rudimentary preventive and condition monitoring checks while running. These checks can include temperature, flow, throughput, fill level, pressure and filter cleanliness – *set up in an interactive "go/no go" style that lends itself perfectly to a regular operator check* (see Figure 3-1). This type of "go/no go" check only requires paperwork in the form of a work request when a "no go" state is in effect.

Take, for example, a pre-RCM PM work order that might have instructed a maintainer to check and record all gauge pressures. This would not just be a waste of maintenance resources – *the maintainer also would have to know the upper and lower safe operating window (SOW) limit for every gauge if a situation were to be immediately averted.*

Recording every good pressure reading in the CMMS history is meaningless and a waste of resources when it comes to data input. Marking each gauge with a HI/LO or Min/Max line to indicate the safe operating window (SOW) now allows any person viewing the instrument to tell if the needle is in the safe or "go" position between the lines, in which case no further action is required or taken. If, however, the needle is outside the SOW mark lines, or in a "no go" state, the operator contacts the supervisor who immediately raises a work request for maintenance to attend the pending situation. Because of the RCM FMEA analysis, maintenance knows right away what the problem root cause could be and activates a planned work order in response to the event condition.

RCM, which advocates autonomous maintenance work by operators (total productive maintenance – TPM), is a perfect catalyst in building and cementing autonomous operator maintenance as a first-level maintenance approach, wherein the operator becomes the true machine guardian on a daily basis. Once a comfortable maintainer/operator working relationship is established, more complex PM-styled tasks, such as lubrication and filter changeouts, can be engineered into the operator-based maintenance program. In Figure 4.2 operator-based maintenance is shown dovetailing into the core element of the maintenance process.

Maintenance/Production Management Alignment

Aligning the maintenance and production management teams to work in partnership is achieved through communication, respect, and recognition of each other's goals and objectives. Both parties collaborate to harmonize the planning and scheduling of the production process and maintenance activity in the best interests of the asset.

As both departments own the equipment in different ways, both compete for "alone" time with the equipment. Unfortunately, if both agendas are not harmonized, the equipment will suffer and both departments will lose.

The interactive input/output information required of both departments in order to prepare and schedule weekly forecasts and daily work schedules effectively is depicted in Figure 4.3. In both cases, monthly and weekly schedule forecasts are being built on an ongoing basis, and being used as "best guesstimates" for assessing and managing resource requirements. From these forecasts come the daily schedules that are usually 70% to 95% accurate – *and which should be just flexible enough to allow for minor unforeseen changes.* To synchronize these daily schedules, both maintenance and production must agree, through the RCM process, what point in an asset's condition dictates an uncontested responsive event in which both the maintenance and production planning and scheduling departments will work together in the asset's interest alone.

The input–output model demonstrated in Figure 4.3 shows how the maintenance department can assist production staff by providing a series of documents that include: a daily asset problem report spelling out any triggered alarm conditions and found "no go" exceptions that require planning and scheduling; a status report of unfinished or "carryover" work from a previous day or shift; a report-driven form with the fault codes marked on the work orders to show the percentage of non-maintenance-caused equipment failures (i.e., operator error, loading errors or jamming, overloading, etc.); and an

Figure 4.2: Maintenance/production interaction pyramid.

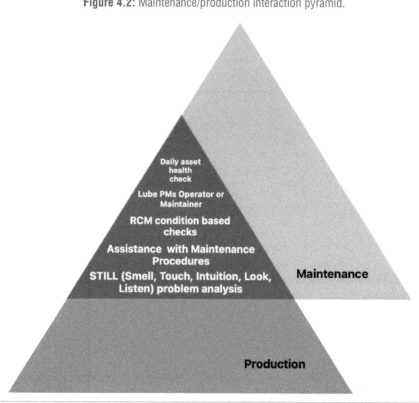

equipment availability report. The production department can further assist maintenance staff through the provision of a report detailing any pending product changeover or retooling event from which maintenance can take the forced downtime opportunity to plan and schedule backlog or pending work on that equipment. Production will also assist maintenance by providing reports on raw material problems, equipment incidents and any work requests. Getting together on a daily basis allows the information transfer and the setting of an almost fixed daily schedule. The end product of this open relationship delivers equipment reliability and availability that in turn can translate directly into sustainable throughput and quality.

Conclusion

When a cooperative partnership environment is created between maintenance and production/operations teams, levels of appreciation for each other's role

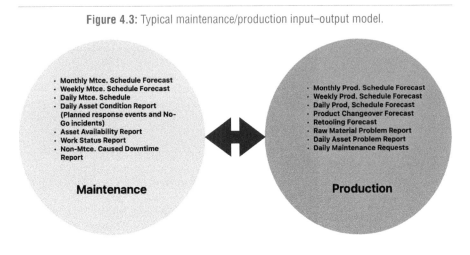

Figure 4.3: Typical maintenance/production input–output model.

is elevated significantly, resulting in an effective maintenance approach that delivers consistent throughput at a high level of quality.

5

Inter-department Partnership Maintenance and Engineering Group

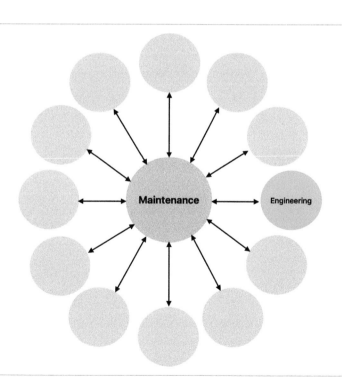

Although it is not always thought so, the engineering department is a close relative of the maintenance department. Examining each other's role in the context of equipment life cycle management portrays a definitive, closely related directive that requires a partnership approach to both mandates.

Maintenance is charged with the primary role of providing equipment availability, reliability and capacity (throughput) in accordance with the engineering and production design specifications on a day-to-day basis. Engineering is charged with the primary role of designing and developing equipment to fit the needs of the production department or client that will deliver a prescribed throughput performance in a reliable manner. Furthermore, the equipment must be both operable and easily maintainable.

More recently, great strides have been achieved in amalgamating technical effort through the introduction of the reliability department, *wherein reliability engineers and predictive maintenance technicians dovetail the two departments into a cohesive partnership.* The partners focus specifically on increasing equipment reliability and availability of both new and legacy equipment through increased understanding of equipment failure and the incorporation of reliability centered maintenance principles. Companies that have achieved this advanced partnership state have understood and acknowledged that both partners' roles constantly overlap, requiring mutual exchange of information on a continual basis to realize both mandates and deliver significant increases in equipment availability, reliability (life cycle), and throughput.

As with any successful relationship, both parties must understand and state what they expect from the relationship, then work together on mapping the input and output instruments that will deliver on those expectations, e.g., meetings, workflow, standardized operating procedures or guidelines, informational reports, budgets, tools, skills, etc. Once mapped, both sides must commit to a management action plan and work through the process, making adjustments as the relationship progresses.

The following complaints are typical of the kind that must be addressed in this relationship:

Complaint #1

Maintenance: *"The only time engineering involves us is when they hand us the keys to the new equipment, at which time they believe their job is finished."*

Engineering: *"We've tried numerous times to involve maintenance in the design and commissioning process of new equipment, yet every time they are either too busy, unprepared or unable to specify their needs."*

Solution...

Too many times, performing a simple maintenance task is made difficult due to poor access, or having to shut down and lock out the equipment. unnecessarily. These incidences can be avoided through effective dialogue between the maintenance and engineering departments in the early design stage.

Engineers are schooled from the beginning on all facets of operator ergonomic design, but rarely maintainer design. Many engineers are unaware of designing for maintenance prevention using a perimeter-based maintenance (PBM) design in which all basic preventive maintenance (PM) measures and change points such as lubricant add/change access, filter change access and predictive maintenance (PdM) measurement points are brought to the machine's perimeter. This allows maintenance (or operators, in a total productive maintenance – TPM environment) to perform proactive work while the equipment is running in production mode.

Adopting guard designs that allow access in less than 30 seconds can reduce redundant maintenance work unbolting guards by hours, freeing up precious resource time. If, however, engineering actively solicits the assistance of maintenance in the early design process, maintenance must commit to the process and provide the services of a maintenance planner who is acutely aware of the access and replacement problems.

New equipment acceptance sign-off at the machine builder's plant and on-site commissioning are great opportunities for a maintenance and engineering partnership to work together toward common goals. Often a new equipment specification requires the original equipment manufacturer (OEM) to deliver a set of working drawings accompanied by a set of preventive maintenance (PM) job plans.

Unfortunately, most OEM PM plans are too generic, not taking into account the recipient's work culture or the operating conditions under which the equipment will perform. These stock PM plans can be traded for much more valuable OEM engineering time by inviting the OEM engineer(s) to take part in a maintenance-department-conducted RCM failure analysis process on the new equipment – PRIOR to receiving the equipment on site. When the equipment is being commissioned, the job plans can be verified while both the reliability engineers and maintainers familiarize themselves with the machine.

Complaint #2

Maintenance: *"When specifying new equipment components such as bearings, controls, chains, gearboxes, etc., why does every engineer have to specify similar, yet different components? Don't they realize this leads to the stocking of multiple similar parts and unpredictable failure patterns?"*

Engineering: *"If the maintenance department is unhappy about the components we specify, why can't they make the effort to inform us on items they prefer, with a reasonable justification for their choice?"*

Solution...

Both parties will receive tremendous benefits from a consolidation and standardization process in which maintenance, repair and overhaul (MRO) items known to deliver consistent reliability are documented. Developing a shared preferred-parts and component-specification listing book in which parts are recognized and listed according to reliability, maintainability and life cycle, is crucial for building and maintaining equipment that can be trusted.

In the parts book, each part is categorized as it would be in the CMMS or EAM maintenance management inventory module. Each part would include, as a minimum, a photograph of the item, item description, OEM #, corporate inventory identification # (if used), vendor #, and item price. Reliability data used to justify the item listing primarily includes mean time between failure (MTBF) reports, cost of downtime associated with item failure and item maintenance replacement cost (item cost + total labor cost).

Examining each other's role in the context of equipment life-cycle management portrays a definitive, closely related directive

This listing book will also benefit the Purchasing and Inventory departments—who are able to reap cost savings through the setup of preferred vendors and the reduction of MRO inventory requirements. At the same time, this approach promotes familiarity with both maintenance components and component maintenance.

Complaint #3

Maintenance: *"When capital budgets get cut, the first system to be eliminated on new equipment is always the lubrication system."*

Engineering: *"Maintenance performs manual lubrication throughout the rest of the plant, what's their problem?"*

Solution...

An engineered lubrication approach is crucial to achieving moving equipment reliability. Automated lubrication systems deliver up to three times the life cycle of manually lubricated bearings. In order to protect and justify an automated lubrication system, the maintenance department must provide lubrication-failure-related data through fault code analysis of lubrication related failures tracked and reported within the CMMS program.

Industrial lubrication education is crucial for both maintenance and engineering, in order for these departments to be able to better understand and facilitate how to apply a truly efficient failure prevention program.

6

Inter-department Partnership Maintenance and Accounting Group

---

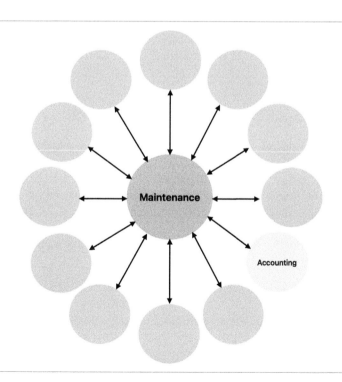

Interested or not, most of us are becoming quite familiar with the concept that "accounting makes the world go around." In recessionary global economic times, corporate fiscal restraint is inevitable, making it tough to push new initiatives to the starting gate and, more importantly, to defend spending on initiatives already in motion.

In both business and personal lives, good accountancy is essential for well-being. It also provides early warning for any needed change to protect that state of well-being. When affairs are awash in red ink, it is difficult to approach any activity in a proactive manner.

Many business decisions are based on simple accountancy criteria requiring validated answers to such questions as:

- What is the total cost?
- What is the return on investment (ROI)?
- Are we within budget?
- Can the budget be cut?

As with every other corporate department billing to a cost center or project, the maintenance department must provide answers to the accounting department – the holder of the corporate purse. These answers are what justify each application for capital expenditure, budget expansion or simple budget retention!

Defining Roles

For most maintenance practitioners, the perception of a maintenance/accounting relationship does not exceed recording and passing along time and material expenses against a G/L (general ledger) account code number, from which an annual maintenance budget may be formulated. Often, the accounting department's perception of maintenance is equally vague. That's because accounting may perceive maintenance purely as a statement of debit against the corporate ledger – which is a legacy of historically having been viewed as a cost center and rarely as a profit center.

If maintenance is to be judged fairly and have any chance of receiving reasonable access to scarce funds, it must define a proactive role in the maintenance/accounting departmental relationship through exploration within the following areas:

- Work with the accounting department to determine any relevant financial information and data useful to facilitating accounting activities, currently collected as part of the CMMS data, and deliver weekly or monthly reports from the CMMS. Such financial information can include monies spent on parts, internal labor, external labor, by project, account code, contractor, etc.

- Determine how maintenance can support accounting in its preparation of budget planning. This can include forecasting PdM and PM contracts with third party contractors, investigation of preferred supplier contracts and vendor managed inventories (VMI) arrangements. Figure 6.1 shows a vendor managed fastener inventory in an automotive engine plant that provided increased parts availability at a fraction of the cost to purchase and manage.
- Work with accounting to determine ROI parameters required to ensure successful submissions of cost/benefit analysis reports for special funding or budget extensions.
- Include the accounting department in all relevant maintenance communications.

Figure 6.1: Vendor managed fastener inventory in an automotive engine plant.

While it is the maintenance department's role to furnish budget plans to the accounting department, it is the role of the accounting department to assist and provide the maintenance department with quality feedback. Both parties must work together to establish guidelines for budget submissions to ensure submission consistency.

Submission guidelines need to be published and circulated to all accounting and maintenance personnel for future reference.

As with all departmental relationships, it is incumbent upon the maintenance department to learn how the accounting department likes to receive information. The maintenance department may be successful in attracting the favor of upper-level management with an improvement proposal, but unless the accounting figures are complete, and fall within the corporate funding guidelines, the new program or purchase could continue to be nothing more than a proposal.

Past Performance

During the infamous 1990s downsizing era, and the 2020s Covid era, the majority of maintenance departments were subjected to deep budget cuts. At that time, most were not ready to defend their programs. Consequently, these departments suffered huge losses in capital expenditure budgets and major losses to maintenance operating funds – for what should have constituted acceptable maintenance expenses.

In the early 1990s, maintenance departments that could articulate in "bottom-line" terms the economic consequence of deferred maintenance as a direct result of the budget slashing didn't merely save their existing budgets. They also were able to capture additional funding for cost-saving initiatives. The tool these successful organizations used was the "cost/benefit analysis" report. This is a report prepared by maintenance to show the impact of maintenance budget cuts.

Any report prepared for the accounting department should allude directly to profit and loss and ROI. By preparing a statement of record and using terms such as "return and investment," the maintenance department does not only reflect good business practices, it also demonstrates a desire to contribute to the corporation's bottom line. Clearly, this type of statement requires upfront research and planning. The effort, though, is worthwhile if your submission receives serious consideration from management and accounting alike.

The Real ROI

To invest in something is to dedicate funds and/or time to a project expected to yield a profit or income – profit or income only commencing once the initial funding or capital has been paid for. The time period between the release of funds and the payback of the funds through the profit or generated incomes is the "return on investment" period. It could range from minutes to years and varies enormously depending upon the application or project. Generally speaking, the faster the ROI period, the better chance the program or purchase has.

Figure 6.2: Typical maintenance/accounting input–output model.

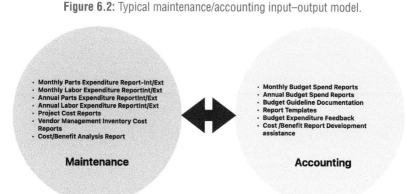

If a maintenance department is to survive recessive times, it must understand ROI and work intensively to understand the fundamentals of a partnership between itself and the accounting department. Figure 6.2 demonstrates some of the input–output requirements needed to foster a healthy partnership.

7

Inter-department Partnership Maintenance and Purchasing Group

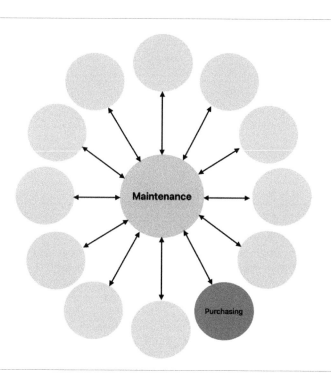

Because of its use of consumable products and need for replacement maintenance repair and overhaul (MRO) inventory items, the maintenance department must requisition and contract through the purchasing department on a daily basis. If equipment reliability is to be assured, the direct working relationship between these departments must be a good one built on an understanding of each other's mandate and clear lines of communication.

The approach toward procuring purchased items varies greatly from organization to organization. Large organizations often support a self-regulated purchasing group, whereas medium to small organizations may rely on maintenance to perform shared purchasing/expediting duties with a single buyer – or even relinquish all purchasing duties to a contracted third-party inventory-management company.

Regardless of the approach, building a workable maintenance/purchasing relationship will depend greatly on how well the following types of complaints are managed.

Complaint #1

Maintenance: *"Purchasing never recognizes the urgency of our purchasing needs, requiring us to take our own measures to ensure the part gets here fast enough, especially on a breakdown job when the production line is down and we need the parts here now!"*

Purchasing: *"Maintenance always tries to side-step the procurement process and expedite parts behind our back, often agreeing to outrageous delivery costs to get things here faster!"*

Solution...

Unfortunately, many maintenance organizations are still purchasing items as a direct result of reactive situations. Maintenance departments that actively engage in proactive maintenance strategies (preventive, predictive, condition-based) linked to the planning and scheduling of maintenance events are better able to provide the purchasing partner with enough lead-time flexibility to procure the part with the best delivery option (no more expensive air freight or taxi delivery charges).

Clearly defining the role(s) of each department (maintenance/purchasing) allows any size organization to map out the procurement business process specific to the organization, as well as set up clear levels of responsibility. Using a template similar to that shown in Table 7.1, both departments must meet to discuss which department is best suited to take on what role based on expediency and ability to perform the role. With roles decided, the workflow

Table 7.1: Role assignment table.

Action	Maintenance	Purchasing

Part Specification
• Technical Specification
   ○ Materials
   ○ Performance
   ○ Size
   ○ Life Expectancy (Reliability)
• Preferred Manufacturer
• Alternate Manufacturer
• Preferred Vendor
• Alternate Vendor		

Stocking Requirements • Min / Max Levels		
Complete Purchase Requisition • Minimum Information Requirements		

Purchase Order
• Complete P.O. Requirements
   ○ Purchase Price
   ○ Delivery Terms
• Assign to Vendor		

Expedite Order		
Maintain Supplier Relationship		

is now diagrammatically mapped indicating the responsible department for each action. This enables both departments to follow a structured approach and develop a working trust with one another.

Complaint #2

Maintenance: *"Purchasing always buys the cheapest product or service it can find."*

Purchasing: *"Maintenance doesn't understand that we have a mandate to continuously reduce purchasing costs."*

Solution...

Establishing MRO-item purchasing programs based on life-cycle costing (LCC) is paramount for reducing downtime costs, equipment repair costs and procurement costs. An LCC program begins with both departments understanding the fundamental difference between price and cost.

When purchasing a replacement MRO item, price is the money paid to receive a quality item FOB (freight on board) at your plant, through regular shipping methods.

Cost is attributed to the equation when additional money is spent without value, as depicted in the following scenarios:

- Price plus additional money for emergency shipping.
- Price plus additional money spent to administer and wait for the return of defective, inferior quality items.
- Price plus additional money spent for accelerated replacement and incurred downtime costs of less expensive, inferior quality items (lower cost items with lower mean time between failure [MTBF] life-cycle reliability ratings).

Purchasing the least expensive item may make sense initially when buying on price alone, as indicated in the Figure 7.1 example below.

Figure 7.1: Buying parts on lowest initial price vs. total life cycle cost doesn't take into account the cost of changing out less expensive, but possibly low quality, parts over time.

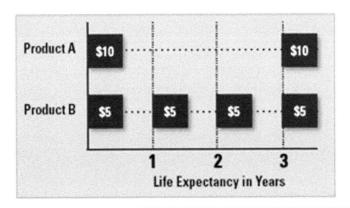

Product A, priced at $10, is twice the price of the $5 Product B. Purchasing Product B over A gains an immediate 50% price saving.

However, taking life-cycle expectancy into account changes the scenario considerably.

Product A has a life expectancy of three years, whereas Product B is a lower-quality manufactured part with an expected life expectancy of only one year. Over a three-year period, Product B is changed out three times compared to Product A, which actually increases the purchase price by 50% over the life-cycle of the more expensive part (1 × $10 expenditure vs. 3 × $5 [$15] expenditure).

Furthermore, purchasing the lower-quality Product B incurs two more sets of additional costs associated with downtime of the equipment, maintenance replacement costs, purchasing administration costs, work order administration costs and inventory management costs over the life cycle of Product A.

Working together to understand and make buying decisions based on life-cycle costing dramatically reduces operations, maintenance and purchasing costs.

Complaint #3

Maintenance: *"Purchasing never seems to purchase the right part."*

Purchasing: *"Maintenance never gives us the correct information to order in the correct part."*

Solution...

Once again, clear lines of communication are vital to attaining mutually desired outcomes. Setting up a minimum information requirement for the purchase requisition, preceded by a detailed part specification standard, as outlined in the Table 7.1 template, will significantly reduce the chances of an incorrect part purchase.

Complaint #4

Maintenance: *"We always get blamed for downtime."*

Purchasing: *"Downtime is not a purchasing problem."*

Solution...

Downtime is everybody's problem. This becomes more apparent when a value stream map is created for the organization depicting inter-department input/output relationships. Taking a facilitated approach, both maintenance and purchasing must work together to become consistent in their methods of procuring and using parts. We already have seen that purchasing parts based on LCC can significantly reduce downtime – something that is brought about through understanding and collaboration between maintenance and purchasing. Other collaborative acts resulting in cost reduction can include:

- Initiating a preferred vendor or supplier program based on quality products, service, delivery and reasonable pricing policy.
- Developing a parts specification book based on existing preferred parts and vendors that have historically shown good life-cycle tendencies.
- Involving purchasing in maintenance planning and scheduling meetings.

Examining typical complaints from the perspective of both partners leads to the formulation of a workable approach that allows maintenance to focus on delivering equipment availability and reliability, and purchasing to focus on procuring products that deliver the best value for the least amount of expenditure.

8

Inter-department Partnership Maintenance and Human Resources (HR) Group

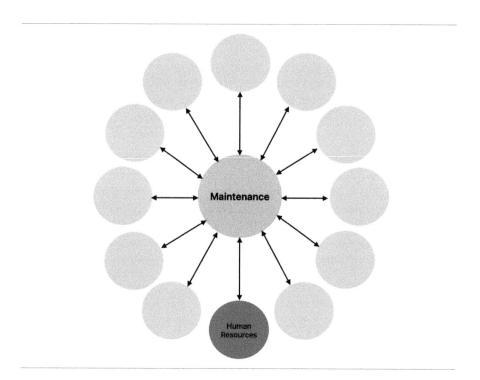

The human resource represented by a company's workforce is arguably the most valuable asset a company possesses. Ironically, to an investor, corporate wealth and value is counted in terms of the current bank balance, order book, inventory and current physical asset value.

In reality, rarely is a price or value tag associated with the workforce and its experienced knowledge of the corporate business – and its intimate working relationship with the processes, procedures and equipment used to deliver an end product. On the other hand, one of the things that successful and sustainable businesses understand is that without a quality human resource working to manage its assets, a company will quickly flounder, or worse yet, cease to exist. That's especially true with regard to the human resource element of a maintenance department.

In many companies, maintainers begin their professional lives with several thousand hours of on-the-job training coupled with formal classroom attendance. They then move on to accumulate a wealth of experience and knowledge regarding business processes, manufacturing operations and the general and idiosyncratic nature of many individual pieces of equipment running in unique environments within their respective companies. Whenever an organization loses a maintenance person, be it through lay-off or career move, the company is losing one of its most valuable assets.

When it comes time to replace a maintainer, the responsibility of finding a similar skilled replacement is most likely to fall on the shoulders of the human resources (HR) department. The new hire can be attained in two ways, either through the direct hiring of a similar experienced individual from outside the company, or through an effective upgrading and training of existing/new staff.

Not every company will have an actual HR department, though. In this case, it is common to designate a person(s) with some real understanding of the job required of the new employee to perform in an HR role. That designated person often is a maintenance superintendent/manager or engineering manager. Regardless of who performs the HR function, it behooves the maintenance department to establish a working relationship with HR personnel and develop a team approach to both hiring and training of maintenance staff.

Including HR on your Team

The HR department can be a wonderful asset to a maintenance department as it has the ability to facilitate many programs on behalf of maintenance. In order to function effectively, an HR department must be cognizant of both long- and short-term corporate and maintenance plans, needs and requirements, which calls for it to be open to establishing positive working relationships. HR assistance to maintenance will most often materialize in the following areas:

- Job descriptions
- Hiring Training programs – individual and group
- Apprenticeship programs
- Compensation/incentive packages.

Job Descriptions

Just as a piece of equipment is designed to a working specification for its intended use within the company, each job position needs to be described in terms of the role the position plays in the organization, and the expected responsibilities each position must shoulder. Job descriptions, or specifications, describe minimum skill requirements and accreditations, skills update expectations and basic responsibilities that need to be met for each job and level of position unique to the corporate culture. Meeting and surpassing these specifications are usually a condition of employment – and are used as a requirements template for hiring new individuals and setting up department training programs.

A job description is an important requirement for any position because it sets down a series of guidelines that lets each individual know exactly what is expected of him/her. The HR department is able to use many job description templates and work with maintenance to develop relevant job descriptions that reflect the unique needs of your departmental culture.

Hiring

When hiring is required, the HR department is the right agency to perform all but the final interview process and deliver to the maintenance a suitable candidate – or candidates – to meet the department's requirements. This unburdens maintenance management personnel, allowing them to get on with the job of maintenance management.

Training Programs

Whenever a new hire, process, methodology, technology or corporate direction is introduced, training will be required. Training programs are best when they are designed and planned to meet both individual and group needs. The HR department works together with the maintenance department to determine training content and delivery. Maintenance schedules the team members who are to receive the training.

Apprenticeship Programs

Ever more important in these days of an aging expert workforce is the fact that many companies are unaware that they may be eligible to set up apprenticeship programs. The HR department is able to broker such programs with State and Federal authorities – as well as set up any suitability audits. Companies with existing apprenticeship programs will likely already be using the HR department to coordinate and administer these programs on maintenance's behalf.

Compensation/Incentive Packages

In addition to dealing with routine compensation, vacation and sick-pay issues, the HR department will usually be closely associated with the development and administration of any corporate or department incentive programs (often in the form of gifts or money) for valid cost reduction suggestions and additional compensation for skills acquired, etc.Maintenance and the HR department must clearly communicate with one another and draw upon each other's experience and strengths to put together a valid set of deliverables that reflects the interests of both departments and the corporation as a whole. Keep in mind, however, that the terms of this partnership won't necessarily be carved in stone. Changing market conditions and corporate restructuring will dictate ongoing and ever-changing relationship requirements.

9

Inter-department Partnership Maintenance and Sales Group

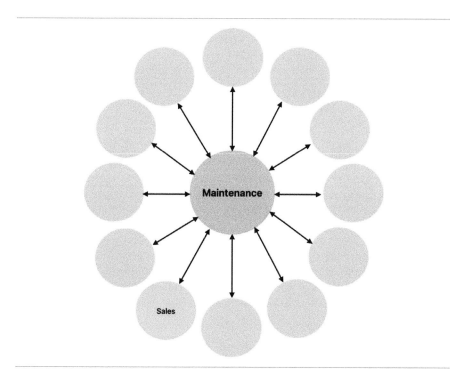

"ABC Corporation of Smalltown, USA, today announced a manufacturing sales order worth over $100 million…"

Such announcements are commonplace in today's business press, leaving little doubt that the sales and marketing department are still revered as corporate heroes when a large sales order is closed. Getting that order to the customer, however, as ordered, on time and with first-time quality requires the effort of many unsung heroes within the plant.

From the post-war 1950s to the 1980s, North American corporate philosophy surrounding the sales process often was "close the sale and we'll worry about design, quality and delivery later." Since many sales were closed in a wine and dine forum, and in a somewhat indiscriminate consumer culture of the time that tended to be accepting of poor design, quality and delivery, countless corporations were successful in spite of themselves.

That all changed when the Japanese singlehandedly raised the bar, having been attributed largely with the responsibility for raising consumer awareness and expectations surrounding quality and service throughout the 1970s and 1980s. This state of affairs finally forced the North American industrial giants into compete mode by the 1990s. New heightened consumer awareness resulted in an intelligent customer who was unafraid to demand quality products at reasonable prices, delivered on time. Competing in this new world order forced many corporations to rethink their sales strategies.

A Renewed Sales Approach

To be considered a viable contender in today's marketplace, a corporation must attain quality assurance certification. Many customers demand ISO 9000 or TS 16949 certification (quality assurance through audited documentation and procedural control to a defined international standard) as a contract bidding prerequisite; more recent standards such as the ISO 14001 Environmental standard, the ISO 55001 Asset Management Standard and the ICML 55.1® Lubrication Management standard have been added

With ISO/QS 9000 certification, the customer is assured that a qualified maintenance program is in effect and also that manufacturing equipment is being maintained to a specified level of reliability. Through this link, the maintenance department is now established integrally with the sales department.

Building on this newly established integration, the modern-day sales approach utilizes a corporate team effort to put together a winning sales proposal. This sales process calls for the salesperson to listen and document the customer's requirements exactly, so that these requirements can then be reviewed by a multi-faceted manufacturing and sales team comprising members of the finance, engineering, production, purchasing and maintenance departments. Because many sales contracts contain penalty clauses for poor quality and poor delivery, the sales team must ensure corporate capability to attain and maintain a sustained level of production throughput for the duration of the sales contract. This only can be assured by the maintenance department.

Further links between maintenance and the sales force have recently been established through the implementation of lean manufacturing initiatives in which the sales department is no longer called upon to fire-sell surplus "made for inventory" product. Instead, sales are made intimately aware of current long-term/short-term surplus manufacturing equipment capability that can be tapped into and sold competitively with high profit margins and low manufacturing cost in a pull manufacturing environment.

Maintenance Facilitating the Sales Process

Although maintenance rarely involves itself in the sales process, it can assist in the sales effort through the provision of reliable equipment performance information, such as:

The throughput capability report: This covers the manufacturing equipment or line intended to produce the new parts. This is essential information in determining the ability to deliver the requested product volumes. Through the process of analyzing the specified equipment maintenance history, a detailed downtime record is used to compare against the machine's design throughput figure, so that a true throughput measure can be predicted. If the throughput requirement is more than the design capability of the plant in question, alternate manufacturing requirements will be needed to provide quality and delivery.

The maintenance cost report: Once again, knowing what equipment will be used to manufacture the product helps the maintenance department establish past maintenance costs for the equipment in question. These cost figures are then averaged out and a projected maintenance cost can be established for the proposed production contract term. Such projections allow the sales department to accurately calculate operation and manufacturing costs. In turn, controlled costs allow corporations to lower profit margins and be more competitive.

The maintenance health report portfolio: Standard maintenance health reports, such as availability, reliability, PM completion, overall equipment effectiveness, etc., are all excellent reports for the sales department to have in its possession.

Providing these reports are favorable; they can be used within a sales presentation to bolster confidence in the corporation's ability to deliver the required goods and services being bid on to potential and actual customers.

In the course of the sales process, maintenance may also be called upon to directly interface with potential customers and provide them with a tour of the maintenance facilities, as well as present an overview of the maintenance process.

The Benefits

Establishing a partnership with the sales department allows the maintenance department to once again be recognized as an entity within the corporation. Being aware of pending contracts lets maintenance better plan any equipment maintenance and overhaul requirement so as to be ready for the production contract in the event the sales department is successful. Involvement in the front end of the sales process also allows maintenance to keep in check the possibility of "overselling" the plant design capacity. Inattention to this element can accelerate maintenance demands quickly, increasing equipment downtime and, ultimately, leading to corporate losses, often blamed squarely on the maintenance department shoulders.

10

External-department Partnership Maintenance and Contracted Service Providers

---

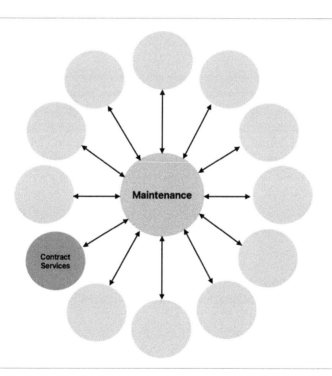

There probably is no maintenance department in the country that hasn't engaged the services of a contractor, or specialty services provider, in the past 12 months. How was your experience?

Past experience with outside assistance usually dictates how you approach your next contractual relationship with an outside labor source. Most of us are likely to remember the negative experiences far and above the positive ones, prompting us to be extra cautious and somewhat jaded at the prospect of working with a new service partner.

Unfortunately, there seems to be an abundance of service providers who are too eager to "stretch" the truth about their capabilities and, in a price conscious world, too willing to cut corners and offer a price-beating alternative. These companies are prone to deliver poor quality and readily sour the partnership experience, never to be invited to quote on a second job. Doubtless we are all aware of the sweetness of a good price – and the bitterness of the true cost when the service falls short of expectations.

Quality work is about setting and surpassing scope-of-work expectations. It is about NOT cutting corners, using quality materials and, above all, dealing with service providers that use personnel who communicate well, are personable, highly competent, trained and experienced. You and your co-workers certainly will recognize many or all of these attributes in your favorite service provider(s).

These days, many companies are actively restructuring their labor pool through redundancy or attrition, with many maintenance departments forced to utilize contract labor to supplement their present understaffing or loss of technical expertise. With utilization of contract labor and specialty service groups, which include trainers, management consultants, OEM technicians, preventive and predictive service providers on the rise, following a few simple rules can assure a maintenance department of having a positive experience, every time.

Rule 1: Establish specialty service provider use guidelines

Working together to take stock and document the current ability and level of expertise of the internal skilled labor pool, both maintenance and human resources can assess and match this capability against present and future plant work requirements.

- **High-demand skilled work** within the current capability of the internal staff should not be contracted out. This work would include general millwright and electrical work.
- **Low-demand work** requiring a high level of expertise, such as overhead door, roof work, training, audit assessment, etc., is a good candidate for the use of specialty service group partnerships.

- **Marginal work** such as heating, ventilating and air conditioning (HVAC) can be negotiated depending on the internal expertise level. Total workload (backlog) also will play a role in determining what type of work can be taken on by internal or contract labor.

Establishing such a guideline document can allow management, unions and workforce to agree on when specialty service providers are to be used.

Rule 2: Establish a value-added specialty service provider relationship

Quality service providers may not come in with the best price, but usually will work hard to sustain a long-term working relationship. In doing so, most are open to delivering additional value-added services for little or no extra cost.

For example, competent and knowledgeable service providers are employed for their expertise; this can be "tapped" into by asking and expecting the service provider to perform the task requirement, and at the same time perform on-the-job training by allowing a maintenance department employee to observe and assist. This type of strategy is especially effective with apprentice training or specialty training of predictive maintenance technologies.

Other value-added services that can be expected from contractors are such things as 24/7 "on call" availability and reduced billing rates for blanket purchase orders.

Rule 3: Establish a specialty service provider management policy

Managing specialty service partnerships should not differ greatly from managing internal resources in that work assignments must be controlled through the work order management system. The service provider's work assignment must be stated clearly, and the work estimated for materials and time requirements. The service provider's performance is based on variance of estimate and completed work quality.

Once the work is complete, prior to closing the work order, this document is used to collect all relevant comments and references to any contractor check-sheets, to check and assure work quality and to compare work done against the invoice statement before payment is released.

A service provider's daily charge rate may initially appear as significantly higher than internal resource rates (often used as an argument against using outside assistance). The decision to use outside service providers, however, must be assessed on their value and judged on timeliness of work completion, work quality, rarity of use (their expertise may only be required 2–3 times per year, or less) and cost of specialty tools used by a provider (an infrared thermographer might use an imaging system worth more than six figures; a consultant might use templates and intellectual property that cost hundreds of thousands of dollars to develop).

Win/Win/Win

Use of a specialty service provider must be a balanced decision. Allowing everyone affected by such a provider to help establish the rules surrounding the use of this type of outside assistance will facilitate a healthy relationship among the workforce, management and contracted party – making for a positive experience!

External-department Partnership Maintenance and The Original Equipment Manufacturer (OEM)

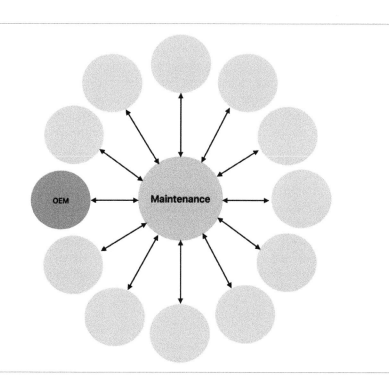

When maintenance is allowed to interact with the plant and production, original equipment manufacturer (OEM), a prosperous relationship for both parties will often ensue. This special partner relationship results in the exchange of first-hand information to the maintenance department that can be used to set up its maintenance approach, in exchange for valuable operational and design feedback to the OEM.

There are seven typical circumstances in which maintenance will interact or communicate with an OEM. These are:

1. New facility or plant process/equipment design.
2. Equipment warranty claims.
3. PM task and schedule generation for original equipment installation.
4. RCM (reliability centered maintenance) analysis of existing and new equipment installations.
5. Implementation and use of proprietary software and diagnostic tools.
6. OEM training using the OEM operations and maintenance manual.
7. Equipment and operational systems updates.

New Production Equipment Design

With increased awareness of life-cycle management costs and the validity of the maintenance process, many purchasing and engineering departments now invite their maintenance departments to assist in the development of new equipment design and operational specifications. Allowing maintenance a voice in this development stage can translate into an improved design focused on delivering increased reliability and quick maintenance turnaround.

Specifying and building equipment with known reliable components (power transmission, electrical, lubrication systems, fasteners, etc.) could marginally increase initial build expense – *but will pay back over the equipment's life span through reduced downtime caused by premature component failure and reduced component stocking expense.* Equipment designed to be maintained with visual management systems that give instant tangible feedback on the equipment's condition, as well as for quick access and component change capability, will drastically reduce set-up time and minimize the mean time to repair (MTTR).

Production Equipment Warranty Claims

Many corporations lose out on new equipment warranties. Misunderstanding of warranty commencement date, warranty duration and terms, alongside poor documentation of failure occurrences during the warranty period, can often result in maintenance paying for a premature failure that should have been back-charged to the OEM as a warranty claim.

Establishing usable warranty parameters requires the OEM and maintenance user to agree upon and document the warranty start date; is this a defined time period from the date of shipment, date of arrival on site or date of signed-off commissioning? Most companies believe it to be the commissioned date and are shocked to find out later it was the shipping date. This is even more disconcerting when the equipment is commissioned past the warranty time period.

The OEM partner fully understands it has a responsibility to support the equipment user at different levels. Maintenance is one of those levels.

Although most equipment typically operates under a one-year warranty period on all mechanical components, electronic components may carry only a 90-day warranty. The maintenance department must be part of the warranty discussions so such items can be marked in the CMMS equipment register and acted upon. Otherwise, maintenance might have to pay for a repair that is not its responsibility.

When exercising a warranty claim, maintenance can facilitate the process by providing the OEM with an up-to-date work log account and relevant digital photos or video of the warranty claim component or area. This information can be immediately relayed electronically to the OEM and an accelerated warranty decision can be made.

PM Tasks and Schedules for Existing Equipment

When setting up a preventive job task for an existing piece of equipment that has no maintenance manual on file, the maintenance department can contact the OEM to request a copy of an original manual and typical PM task information. If the equipment is old, the OEM will at the very least have the knowledge to assist in the setting up of preferred basic PM routines for the equipment.

RCM (Reliability Centered Maintenance) Analysis of Both Existing and New Equipment Installations

A preferable approach to the previous scenario when setting up a PM program for existing or new installations is to adopt a reliability centered maintenance approach and invite the OEM to take part in the RCM analysis process to build PMs based on the ambient condition factors and consequences of failure.

Implementation and use of Proprietary Software and New Tools

Most of today's equipment will use some form of computer control accompanied with proprietary software that can help in diagnosing equipment breakdowns and slow-downs. OEMs can also provide other specialty tools to operate, troubleshoot and repair equipment failures. Tools such as diagnostic meters, hand tools (wrenches, screwdrivers) and power tools will all carry a warranty – *and some will require ongoing support from the OEM through the learning phase of product use.*

Training

With the purchase of a new product comes a need for training. In the case of maintenance diagnostic tools and maintenance software, the training requirement is best addressed before the equipment arrives on site. Unfortunately, many corporations wrongly believe that because a machine is built up from a selection of electrical and mechanical components that the maintenance staff does not require training. (These same decision-makers would shudder if their car dealers' auto mechanics were not trained on their latest automobile purchases!)

Equipment is made up of *independent* and *interdependent* systems that the maintenance staff must first understand before moving to the component level they understand so well. An excellent opportunity for maintenance training is during the commissioning process. By allocating a maintenance representative to the commissioning team, valuable "on the job" relevant training can be attained at no extra cost. The designated maintainer can later be used to train other maintainers.

Equipment and Operational Systems Updates

Periodically, equipment will receive updates to both its mechanical, and more specifically, its electronic/electrical systems. Updates and improvements could mean a change to the PM task and require additional training.

Once a piece of equipment is sold, the OEM fully understands it has a partnership responsibility to support the equipment user at different levels. Maintenance is one of those levels – *and a very important one.* It is up to maintenance, however, to communicate its need to the OEM partner.

12

External-department Partnership Maintenance and Parts Vendor/Suppliers

---

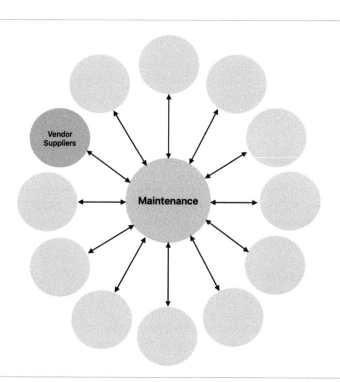

Whenever the cost of a repair is calculated, it typically is broken down into two specific components – parts and labor. The stocking of maintenance, repair and overhaul (MRO) parts in preparation for a planned or unplanned maintenance event typically necessitates ongoing partnerships with multiple vendors. The set-up and continued management of these types of ongoing partnerships will have a tremendous impact on equipment availability, reliability and cost of maintenance.

Deadly Sins

"Machine down, waiting for parts." If this is a familiar statement found on your returned work orders or daily maintenance schedule, you are likely working in a highly reactive maintenance environment.

Unfortunately, when equipment downtime is being experienced as a result of the part(s) unavailability, the tendency is to pay premium prices for both parts and delivery. For example, have you ever been in a situation in which a crucial part is not available locally, forcing you to air-freight and taxi a non-discounted part into the plant? In a proactive maintenance department, this scenario is viewed as a deadly sin, since travel costs of a part purchased in such a manner significantly compounds the maintenance repair cost.

A second "deadly sin" is associated with maintenance developing the tendency to overstock low-turnover items. Purchased in multiples, these items often are stored in non-controlled, cached inventories (sometimes called "squirrel stocks"), in places like tradesmen toolboxes, equipment cabinets, etc. With annual carrying costs as high as 35 cents on the dollar and prohibitive access to "squirreled" parts, inventory costs easily skyrocket with poor or no return to the maintenance department.

Working to eliminate out-of-stock, overstock and guaranteed delivery of non-stock items (without penalty) requires a defined maintenance/MRO vendor partnership agreement in which each partner understands his/her role in ensuring that parts are "ready to go" at any time.

Establishing Vendor Partnerships

One of the hallmarks of a successful business is a trust-driven relationship between the company and its supplier/vendor base that views those purveyors of goods and services as a natural extension of the company itself.

A basic MRO inventory consists of three major spare part categories:

- **Original equipment manufacturer (OEM) items**: These are proprietary items available only from the machine builder, usually with long lead purchase times.

- **Insurance spares**: The items are inventoried for purposes of due diligence, and required by the corporate underwriter for equipment that could pose high-risk consequences when in a prolonged failed state.
- **Industrial supply items**: These are available "off the shelf" from many different vendors.

Vendor relationships can vary significantly. They depend not only on the willingness of vendors to work with maintenance, but also on the relationship and partnership already established between maintenance and purchasing, which acts as the corporate agent with the vendor.

There are basically four types of partnership agreements in which a maintenance department and parts vendor can engage:

- **The lowest bidder**: This is a common relationship in which the maintenance department, often driven by a strong purchasing department mandate, follows a path of least-resistance and acquiesces to the purchase of supplies from the lowest-priced vendor. This method is especially time-consuming in that every item must be individually "shopped," requiring extensive use of the purchasing system. This type of relationship is reactive in nature, not built on trust. Furthermore, it is not conducive to building long-term relationships with vendors.

  One of the hallmarks of a successful business is a trust-driven relationship between the company and its supplier/vendor base that views these entities as a natural extension of the company itself.

- **The preferred vendor**: When a vendor has established a good, trustworthy service record and a history of fair pricing, it can be considered an excellent candidate for "preferred vendor" status. Such an agreement generally means the vendor receives exclusive selling rights for listed inventory items, for an agreed price, delivery and specified time period. In return for this agreement, the vendor agrees to keep a minimum stock ready for immediate delivery (often from the vendor's premises) at no additional cost to the maintenance department. This partnership agreement promotes consistency of purchasing and supply; allows free exchange through a single blanket purchase order; and reduces or eliminates the carrying costs associated with carrying and managing maintenance inventory.
- **The consignment vendor**: This type of partnership allows the inventory vendor to set up its own shelving and stock items on the company's premises, again at no additional cost to the company. The

maintenance department then simply uses the "free-issue" items as its own, while the vendor accounts for items used on a daily, weekly or monthly time basis, and bills the company for the parts used after the fact. The advantage of this type of partnership is having managed inventory immediately available –for zero capital outlay at a previously agreed upon pricing structure. In return, the vendor receives a term-based, exclusive right-to-sell agreement. Already popular on the basis of free issue style items that include gloves, rags, nuts and bolts, etc., these partnerships rapidly are gaining more ground by offering higher-priced, high use items such as bearings, electrical and power transmission supplies.

- **The hub vendor**: Such a partnership is a radical shift from those listed previously, in that it reflects a performance-based service arrangement in which the vendor operates and controls the entire MRO inventory on behalf of the maintenance department. A single-source vendor acts as an outsource agency and takes responsibility for purchasing, stocking and staging of all MRO inventory. The vendor is rewarded for parts availability and turnaround time – and paid on a monthly basis. The inventory may or may not reside on the plant floor, and could possibly have consignment inventory as part of its make-up.

Get Smart

Whatever type you choose, remember that you want it to be a "smart" one. That's because smart maintenance/MRO vendor partnerships help the maintenance department run smoothly, while reducing carrying costs and working capital expenditure.

13

External-department Partnership Maintenance and Auditors

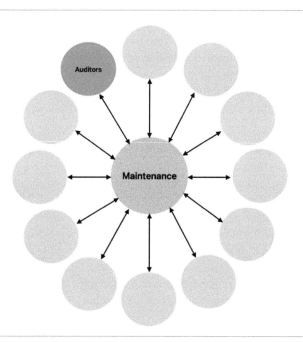

The customs, practices and behaviors exhibited within a workplace are termed "corporate culture," with each corporation, company, even individual departments revealing and immersing themselves in their own unique cultures.

Living and working within a corporate culture rarely allows an individual the opportunity to perform a cultural self-assessment without bias. That old "I can't see the forest for the trees" adage clearly sums up our self-assessment inadequacy. The ability to candidly rate ourselves is hindered for a number of specific reasons:

- Lack of knowledge pertaining to a structured audit process
- Clouding of personal judgment due to internal politics and misunderstandings
- Lack of business process knowledge
- Inability to successfully communicate with personnel at all corporate hierarchical levels.

Thus, to obtain accurate, unbiased "present state" assessments, an organization will seek out and retain, or in the case of mandatory audits and some voluntary ones, "receive" the services of professional auditors.

How and Why Assess?

There are various reasons for assessing the current state of a corporate, company and/or departmental culture, including, for example: regulatory compliance, accreditation compliance, licensing compliance, continuous improvement, change management, etc. Most of these reasons will eventually lead to the services of an auditor.

Because auditors are trained in the audit process and are able to view the corporation or department from the "outside in" – *without bias* – they are better able to deliver a fast, accurate audit assessment. Audits can be divided into mandated and voluntary categories.

- Mandated audits... are compulsory, with the scope of the audit being determined and directed by the regulatory agency performing the audit. Typical mandated audits include: tax audits by the Internal Revenue Service (IRS); validation audits of pharmaceutical or food companies by the Food and Drug Administration (FDA); licensing audits of nuclear power plants by the Nuclear Regulatory Commission (NRC).
- Voluntary audits... are most likely to be self-funded with a self-determined scope. Typical voluntary audits include: ISO certification audits that include ISO 9001 for quality systems, ISO 14001 for environmental systems, ISO 55001 for asset management systems and ICML 55.1® for lubrication management systems. There are also

operational effectiveness audits performed by outside subject matter expert consultants, competition audits for companies competing for awards by judging/jurying committees (the Malcolm Baldridge Quality Award and North American Maintenance Excellence [NAME] Award are two that come to mind).

Audits – *regardless of type* – clearly are an important issue for a business. Since maintenance is an integral part of the business, its methods, processes and results can be subject to scrutiny or audit just like those of other departments – at any time. That said, any audit of a maintenance department will tax the organization's resources. Understanding everyone's role in the process, therefore, will optimize effort.

An organization preparing for an audit may wish to appoint a single person or team of specially trained internal auditors (usually relevant corporate staff trained by a professional audit company) to prepare and perform a mock internal audit "dry run" audit prior to the real event the maintenance department must communicate with the auditor prior to the event. This is done to determine two very critical elements:

1. The audit scope and
2. The auditor's requirements.

What, Where, How Long and By Whom?

Audit scope states exactly what is to be audited. In a mandated audit, the auditor will determine and provide the audit scope. For example, a nuclear power plant applying for an operational license can expect the NRC to determine the entire operation within the audit scope. On the other hand, the scope of an environmental spill audit initially will be confined to the immediate spill area.

In a voluntary audit, the corporation, company or department has the right to choose its auditor. Interviewing auditor(s) for suitability in terms of past experience, industry knowledge and their understanding of YOUR business needs is imperative. If two or more auditor candidates meet your technical needs, choose the one you feel the most comfortable partnering with, securing assurances that "who you see, is who you get" during audit time.

The next step is specifically determining and spelling out the audit scope to the auditor.

In a voluntary audit, the corporation determines exactly what is to be audited. For example, if you are undergoing ISO registration, you may choose to just register a single department, production line or process – not the entire plant. This being the case, the auditor will focus only on the methods, processes and records specific to the running and maintaining of that department, line or process.

In both mandatory and voluntary audits, once the audit scope is determined and understood, the auditor must be interviewed to determine the time and duration of the actual audit and the auditor's requirements. What does he/she want to see? During actual audits, auditors typically have limited time on site. Thus, they often will detail lists of places or items they wish to review during their visits.

Places to see might include the MRO inventory crib or the maintenance tool crib. Items to see might include a work order flow process map or a PM completion report. An auditor might even ask to interview a maintainer on how the maintenance department functions.

The Bright Side?

Fortunately for most maintenance departments, working with an auditor is an infrequent event. When it does occur, effective communication with the auditor will facilitate the audit process and help place maintenance in a position to grow as a result of the audit findings.

14

Partnering with Technology

Many equate the advent of the modern technology revolution to the introduction in the early 1980s of the personal computers (aka PCs).

Since that time, computerization has dramatically changed the way human beings think and act. Yet, some of us still had to be dragged kicking and screaming into the 21st century and have only recently given in to the "force" and assimilated into the techno paradise that now touches and embraces each of our lives on a minute-by-minute basis.

For the few still in denial, it's difficult to imagine living without an automatic teller machine dispensing your money on a 24-hour basis, or trying to purchase a vehicle that is not controlled with more computer power than what put man on the moon. Try to imagine a world without a cellular phone – *have you tried to find a public phone that takes actual money these days?* Where would we be without our "point-and-shoot" cell phone camera systems or our ultra-realistic high-resolution interactive games? Then, of course, let's not forget the information superhighway we call the Internet, which has changed the way we access information, pay bills, make friends and buy and sell stuff!

Similarly, technology has accelerated industry into a "warp-speed-ahead" introduction and continual update of complex computerized asset and information management systems, computerized document management systems, computerized manufacturing control systems and a host of high-tech user-friendly diagnostic equipment. Throughout all of these changes, the maintenance department has been dragged along, often unwillingly, for the ride.

New, Improved Techno-maintenance

To gain recognition as an integral element of the production process, the maintenance department has been forced to drastically change and improve its methods and level of communication. It's done so by building the types of strategic partnerships this book addresses – *with technology playing a significant role in establishing and sustaining these relationships.*

Delivering machine and physical asset effectiveness, availability and uptime has fast become the new maintenance creed. Setting maintenance goals and objectives that dovetail into production/manufacturing goals and corporate goals are concepts that would have been almost laughable 30 years ago. The new and improved maintenance department has entered the era of "techno-maintenance" in which today's maintainer must understand and work with complex equipment designs and control systems that demand a critical thinking approach to troubleshooting, combined with a moderate to high computer skill level.

The modern maintenance department has kept pace through the introduction of maintenance philosophies such as TPM (total productive maintenance) and failure analysis methods used in RCM (reliability centered maintenance), both of which demand the maintenance department to develop partnerships with operators and engineers, and gain an intimate knowledge of the equipment itself – *which requires good data.*

Data remains meaningless until it is discreetly gathered, analyzed and turned into real-time management information using systems such the CMMS (computerized maintenance management system). Data is received whenever a transaction is opened and closed through the work request and work order process. Data is collected real-time through electronically connected "online" condition-based management equipment monitoring systems, and through downloading of interfaced predictive maintenance diagnostic technologies such as infrared thermographic systems, and vibration analysis systems, etc., all used on a daily basis in the majority of today's maintenance and reliability departments.

Lifelong Learning

In the early 1900s, much of the industrial equipment in use was handmade by Victorian-influenced craftsmen who were also required to maintain the equipment. By the 1920s, the mechanization revolution had restructured the way equipment was designed and manufactured – *think of Henry Ford and his Model T, and Frederick Taylor's time/motion studies and Shewhart's Plan, Do, Check, Act methods.* Manufactured components and equipment could be made utilizing machines, and put together on moving assembly lines with every action timed to the second. Maintaining this new manufacturing approach required less of a craftsman's hand and more of a specialist's hand. Accordingly, the maintenance profession began to develop multiple specialties, including: electricity (electrician); steam (steamfitter, stationary engineer); machining (machinist); mechanics (fitter, mechanic, millwright); and metalworking (sheet metal worker, plater, welder).

The new maintenance specialists were collectively called tradesmen. To stay employable, most craftsmen moved into their strongest niche area to be absorbed as one of these new tradesmen. Thus, mechanization gradually phased out the craftsman from the industrial mainstream requirement.

Decades Later

History began repeating itself in the 1980s with the computerization revolution that today continues to move at a blistering pace placing huge demands on traditional tradespersons. With more and more equipment now being designed by computer, built by robots, and run and self-diagnosed by computer control, modern maintenance requirements demand critical thinking skills and computer diagnostic abilities. 25 years into the new millennium, it is easy to see the maintainer's role as one that has evolved from that of a tradesperson to that of an actual capacity assurance technician (CAT).

Today's rapid pace of change demands a modern maintainer be current in both manufacturing and maintenance technologies – *as well as modern maintenance methods and philosophies.* Arguably, the relationship a modern-day maintainer has with technology is one of extreme importance if he/she is to be viewed as a valuable and marketable employee. Luckily, as maintenance professionals, we do not have to write the code for the technology, only invest in understanding how to operate and analyze with the technology.

To reach a level of comfort in our work lives, we must examine and draw upon the comfort with technology that we enjoy in our personal space and lives, and realize they are one and the same. Remember, however, that partnering with technology involves more than simply investing in a computer and "exploring the internet."

Truly partnering with technology involves investment in oneself. Maintainers must invest in themselves through reading books , e-books, online training programs and build one's own maintenance and engineering reference library, either electronic, i.e. that can be accessed by phone or computer, or in print.

Maintenance must familiarize themselves with (and learn how to apply) technology in the workplace.

The payoff to all this? Investing in oneself and staying current in the technology of your profession is a partnership that virtually assures a position in the maintenance environment of the future!

Index